CODE CALM

ON THE STREETS

MENTAL TOUGHNESS SKILLS FOR PRE-HOSPITAL EMERGENCY PERSONNEL

KERRY A. WHITELOCK, D.O.
MICHAEL J. ASKEN, PH.D.

CODE CALM ON THE STREETS

FIRST SUNBURY PRESS EDITION
Printed in the United States of America
September 2012

Trade paperback ISBN: 978-1-62006-108-4

Published by:
Sunbury Press
Mechanicsburg, PA
www.sunburypress.com

Mechanicsburg, Pennsylvania   USA

Preface

We can all appreciate the importance of preventive medicine, the role for clinical pathways and even the entertainment value of esoteric diagnosis, as exemplified by TV character Dr. Gregory House. However, when the public stands in awe of medical expertise, it is emergency care that is the icon of medical skills, procedures, and commitment.

Medical emergencies are dynamic, complex situations that carry the highest expectations to perform optimally. Medical emergencies call for the swiftest and most decisive application of our knowledge and skills. A confident, determined and focused mental state, often termed "mental toughness," is essential for maximal and optimal application of skill.

As eloquently described by the iconic physician Sir William Osler in his words in the next section, "coolness and presence of mind under all circumstances" is a goal and requirement for effective response. Unfortunately, research and experience demonstrate that for many medical personnel, the "code," and any other medical emergencies are highly stressful experiences. Stress can "mess" with your head, and therefore, your actions.

The performance-degrading effects of stress are well-documented. Most of this research is from the hospital setting, an emergency environment that is designed, protected, and equipped to maximize emergency care. When the medical emergency is on the street, though, the calmness and coolness espoused by Osler may be challenged to an extreme degree.

However, too often, the "mental toughness" that is so readily endorsed in many areas of high-stress human performance is not directly developed in emergency care. It is seen as occurring as a "side effect" of training, or even more so, of experience.

But what of those actions and events early in a career before "experience" has been gained? What of the unique or unusual event that is beyond the comfort zone of the standard operating procedures of even experienced personnel?

It is now being recognized in the military and elsewhere that the direct training of mental toughness skills is needed and is the only way to ensure the development of such psychological performance skills and mental readiness. As the famous warrior Sun Tzu stated:

Victorious warriors win first, then go to war. Defeated warriors go to war first and then seek to win.

Code Calm on the Streets seeks to serve as an introduction to directly training the psychological performance skills that comprise mental toughness and maximize performance in high-stress medical emergencies. The integration of psychological skills and technical skills training provides a synergy that can enhance the quality of emergency care for all involved. It is with anticipation and humility that we provide this information to those who provide the highest service to their fellows in the harshest of circumstances for the most humanistic of motivations.

Foreword

How do you focus your inner thought process to maximize your mental abilities to stay calm? How can you best protect yourself against the many distractions and mental hazards in the world of pre-hospital providers? If you are searching for the answers to these questions, then the book in your hands is one you simply must read.

Twenty plus years ago I sat in my first EMT class and heard the following words: "Either you will be able to hack it in this business or you won't. Not everyone is cut out to be an EMT."

At the time I was a young woman intrigued by the challenge to perform under stress. I was looking for the adrenaline and responsibility the job of being a pre-hospital provider would give to me. I had no thoughts of failure. I was hooked from the very start. A class I had taken—simply because of wanting to learn what actions to take in an accident I might happen upon—became the basis of a career.

Over the past twenty two years, I have worn many hats in this profession: from volunteer and paid EMT, to paramedic and EMS educator. It is this last role that has most changed the way I look at the field we are in and those basic premises that were spoken to me so long ago. Yes, I do believe that there are some people who are simply "not wired" to be pre-hospital providers, but I also believe that many students have been misguided and failed by the training, or lack thereof, they receive upon entering the field.

How do we change this? How do you teach calm? As an instructor what can I do to better prepare my students to enter into the world of EMS? How do we develop these students into the kinds of EMTs I would wish to see walk through my door if I were sick or injured? How do you help yourself as provider maximize your skill for excellence? The book you are about to read can help provide those answers.

Drs. Kerry Whitelock and Michael Asken offer a way of shifting our focus from reaction (CISM) to pro-action. Yes, addressing the mental health of our providers *after* they have been exposed to a critical incident is important. But, wouldn't we best be served by shifting the focus to learn how best to respond to these critical incidents before they happen?

Many will clearly recognize the double fatal with children involved, or death of a co-worker as a situation where attention must be paid. Often though, personal critical incidents are what go unnoticed. The code that looks like your grandfather, the miscarriage of a pregnant woman who is due the same time as your wife, the accident where a responder feels they made a mistake—these "personal crisis" calls occur everyday, go unnoticed, and I believe ultimately drive many from our profession. They test our resilience, but they first test our ability to function in the immediacy of the situation.

In the pages of *Code Calm on the Streets* are techniques and mental exercises that can help train the brain to respond in a calm and focused manner. The book allows for mental toughness to be learned so that we may function better in the midst of and, hopefully, be better protected from the stresses of the job. For EMS educators it offers new ways to help our new recruits learn how to face the tasks ahead with more tools in their "mental jump bag." It does the same for you as a provider.

The idea that "knowledge is power" is what I now try to impress upon my new students during their first class. The importance of knowledge and mastery of skills, protocols, ever changing medical information, and our own physical and mental abilities is what will protect us most from the chaos we face every day in the field. We must never believe that we know it all—or that we are inoculated from the dangers and pitfalls of the stress-laden job we do.

This book will provide a base of knowledge for all. For new responders, you will learn a valuable perspective to more quickly maximize your confidence and skills. If you are a veteran provider in this field, you will recognize in the teachings in this book many things that you already innately do in varying degrees. Within the pages you will find ways to hone the skills you already possess and develop new ones. I hope all of you find this book as helpful and interesting as I have. Thank you to all that have "hacked it" and for the services you provide every day.

Stay safe. Stay calm.
Donnel Ruga,
EMS Educator

Table of Contents

Introduction..1

Chapter 1   Fit for Duty: Physical Conditioning
and Mental Toughness.......................6

Chapter 2   Emotional Lights and Sirens: Arousal
and Mental Toughness.....................13

Chapter 3   Mental Alarms: Stress, Fear and
Mental Toughness...........................19

Chapter 4   Mental Diazepam: Arousal Control
and Mental Toughness.....................29

Chapter 5   Mental Scans: Performance-
Enhancing Imagery and Mental
Toughness......................................37

Chapter 6   Mental Scopes: Concentration and
Mental Toughness...........................43

Chapter 7   Mental Prescriptions: Self-Talk and
Mental Toughness...........................50

Chapter 8   Mental Ablations: Negative Thought
Stopping and Mental Toughness.....58

Chapter 9   Mental Clinical Pathways:
Affirmations, Attitude and Mental
Toughness......................................63

References and Resources....................................66

About the Authors...72

Introduction
by Dr. Kerry Whitelock

. . . no quality takes rank with imperturbability . . .
coolness and presence of mind under all circumstances,
calmness amid storm, clearness of judgment
in moments of grave peril.

~Sir William Osler

Fifteen years ago, as I crouched behind a bush providing emergency care to a victim during a sniper attack, adrenaline coursing through my veins, heart pounding, not knowing when the next gunshot would come, I relied on prayer, common sense, determination, and my trauma algorithms to successfully get my patient and me through an incredibly intense situation.

Afterwards, I went through critical incident stress debriefing sessions, which were helpful, but I wondered if, had I received instruction about how to maintain mental toughness during medical emergencies during my formal emergency medical technician (EMT) training, I could have been even more proficient in my patient care duties on that fateful day.

My situation is not unique; all prehospital personnel respond to at least one call during their career that has a significant psychological impact on them. Beyond such unique and transformational experiences, many, if not all, emergency calls are characterized by high demands and high stress. However, EMT and paramedic training programs do not equip pre-hospital personnel with the psychological techniques that emphasize mental toughness, thereby assisting pre-hospital personnel with handling medical emergencies in a competent manner.

Emergency medical services (EMS) literature is now deservedly and fortunately full of studies that discuss the merits and drawbacks of critical incident stress debriefing and delve into burnout and how to define it and its impact on EMS. However, it can be argued that the literature, national EMT and paramedic curricula, and EMS texts do not teach requisite mental toughness skills on the front-end to help responders maximize performance in all the stressful calls they encounter.

Indeed, this missing link of training is well-demonstrated by the following example. During one of my EMT classes, we asked the instructor how he handled the adrenaline so that he could care for the patient. His answer was that "you just handle it." Clearly, pre-hospital personnel deserve a better answer than that, for as the population ages with chronic and multiple conditions, the acuity and complexity of medical emergencies increases, thereby demanding stronger patient care skills from EMTs and paramedics.

The scope and nature of medicine have changed drastically over the years. The nostalgic images Norman Rockwell created of doctors and their patients have been replaced by cutting-edge technology and fast-paced medical care. Pre-hospital personnel are the first link in the chain of medical care, and they need to be prepared to handle anything.

The medical emergency demands the smooth and decisive application of the EMS provider's highest skills and deepest knowledge. Fernandez and colleagues (2008) have written that the practice of emergency medicine involves the management of complex patients in a dynamic and often uncertain environment. Coolness and presence of mind are required in all emergency situations, regardless of experience and whether the skills are recent, remote, or yet to be developed.

The need for competence of psychological skills in other areas of human performance is well-recognized. Lt. Colonel Dave Grossman, a former Army Ranger and accomplished author writes:

> In the end, it is not about the "hardware," it is about the "software." Amateurs talk about hardware, or equipment; professionals talk about software, or training and mental readiness.

Mental toughness is in no way incompatible with clinical sensitivity, empathy, or rapport. In fact, mental toughness is likely to enhance these essential aspects of care because it is defined as:

Possessing, understanding, and being able to utilize a set of psychological skills that allow the effective and even maximal execution and/or adaption and persistence of decision-making and clinical skills learned in training and by experience.

Mental toughness expresses itself in both everyday and high-stress, critical situations. It is accepted that solid preparation can reduce the stress of any situation. Thus, the integration of a mental toughness psychological skills component with medical skills training can enhance care and possibly reduce the potential negative impact of emergency stress on performance and outcomes. Honig and Sultan (2004) write:

Stress survival strategies, including controlled breathing, positive self-talk, and visualization or mental rehearsal trained to a level of confidence and competence, may be critical to both improved performance under stress and increased resilience after a traumatic incident.

Code Calm on the Streets provides the concepts and psychological skills for performance enhancement in a practical way that promotes learning, mastery, and application of physical and decision-making skills to provide an optimal response to managing an emergency situation. This, in turn, enhances the confidence of prehospital personnel in their diagnostic and clinical skills and their approach to a wide variety of patient care situations. Psychological performance skills training for emergency medical situations should include basic concepts and specific techniques.

Basic concepts include an understanding of the following:

3

- The relationship of physical conditioning to cognitive function and performance
- The nature of physical arousal and impact on performance
- Achieving optimal performance states
- The nature of performance stress and the effect of stress on performance
- Situations where arousal needs to be increased or decreased
- The nature of fear and performance
- The effects of stress on thinking
- The effects of stress on group decisions
- The impact of negative thinking and thought suppression

Specific techniques to control stress and enhance performance include:

- Arousal control and self-regulation techniques:
- Concentration enhancement
- Attention control techniques
- Imagery techniques
- Cognitive control techniques
- Negative thought stopping
- Affirmations

Evidence exists to support the effectiveness of each of the components described above. For example, Starr (1987) found that laypeople who underwent a form of psychological skills training called stress inoculation in addition to standard CPR training were less hesitant to use their skills in a test situation and retained a higher percentage of correct skills over time.

The concepts and techniques described in *Code Calm on the Streets* are meant to provide a basis for psychological skills for enhanced performance. Our understanding of what leads to optimal performance is constantly changing, and unique situations call for individualized adaptations of these concepts and techniques. Creative adaptation of the material presented here is fully encouraged.

However, psychological skills training is not a substitute for practice, experience, and other emergency skills training. This material is to be integrated with other training to provide a truly comprehensive approach to the preparation and performance of EMS personnel. Consistent application of these concepts remains crucial to retain maximal effectiveness.

Whether in routine care or emergency situations, each response provides the opportunity for touching and changing the lives of our patients. Hopefully, *Code Calm on the Streets* may help you do this with greater confidence and competence.

Note: For editorial economy, the pronoun "he" will be used exclusively. Its use includes female responders as well, and in no way is meant to minimize or marginalize the considerable elite and heroic contributions of female responders to protecting our communities.

Chapter 1

Fit for Duty:
Physical Conditioning and Mental Toughness

*A man too busy to take care of his health is like a
mechanic too busy to take care of his tools.*

~Spanish proverb

Your body is your most basic piece of equipment. It
needs attention, care, and conditioning. A major focus of
this book is to describe how the mind and body need to
function in synchrony for optimal emergency medical
performance. True confidence and competence are a
combination of physical and mental excellence. We will
focus on exercise, substance/drug use, and sleep in this
chapter on maintaining your most useful piece of
equipment—your body.

Exercise and Physical Conditioning

PHYSICAL IMPACT

In an article (2009) entitled, "The Stress Paradox. The
War on Trauma: Lessons Learned from a Decade of
Conflict," Bruce Siddle wrote:

*Very few professions operate in extreme
environments that also require precise skills; even
fewer have the added stress of saving lives as their
core mission.*

Top physical condition is essential for maximal and
extreme performance. The performance benefits of
conditioning are both physical and psychological.

Exercise can:

- reduce resting heart rate and blood pressure
- decrease ischemia and improve overall cardiac function under stressful conditions
- increase strength, which facilitates moving, rolling, and lifting patients
- decrease risk of injury on the job

Your level of fitness can also directly affect the quality of care you can provide to your patients. Ochoa et al. (1998) studied ICU and ED staff and found that the quality of chest compressions during CPR decreased due to fatigue. Your level of fitness can also directly contribute to your safety, as in dealing with combative, delirious, or psychotic patients.

PSYCHOLOGICAL IMPACT

Exercise also has powerful psychological benefits. Existing in a symbiotic and synergistic relationship and environment, mind and body can significantly enhance performance.

Exercise can:

- increase self-esteem
- decrease anxiety
- increase pain tolerance
- improve memory
- increase resistance and resilience to stress
- increase confidence

An important contemporary physical training concept is that of *functional fitness* or "Functional Conditioning." This approach uses exercises that reflect real world skills of an EMT so that workouts prepare you for the physical requirements of your job. DiNasio (2006) calls this the Law of Exercise Specificity, which emphasizes the importance having exercise mimic the conditions in which an individual functions.

7

Pre-hospital personnel do considerable lifting and maneuvering of patients over varying distances, so your workouts should combine strength training and cardiovascular conditioning to be fully prepared to handle the rigors of the job.

You can use many different techniques to improve your chances of sticking to your exercise routine so that you and your patients benefit from your exercise regimen over time.

Many of these concepts can be found in the model of the "tactical athlete," the idea that public safety personnel are essentially athletes, though the application of their skills is for human benefit rather than competition. An excellent resource for tactical athlete training is the National Strength and Conditioning Association website, www.nsca-lift.org.

Really plan your physical conditioning program. Consider input from a personal trainer. Plan a strategy to insure your compliance with the program; focus on *getting physical and staying physical.* You can improve motivation and compliance with your conditioning program by:

- Charting your exercises and gains (this is especially important when hitting plateaus- points where initial progress slows or seems nonexistent in your program)
- Setting short and long-term goals
- Rewarding yourself daily for achieving goals
- Working with an exercise "buddy" or exercising as a group or team in friendly competition
- Making the conditioning program part of your lifestyle and identifying with it by doing such things

as keeping exercise gear in your car rather than thrown in the back of your closet

- Monitoring your "thinking" about and during your training program—avoiding negative thoughts about exercise—thinking about why exercise is good for you and your performance excellence while you are working out.

Finally, in addition to your gym workouts, include functional conditioning. For example, if you work primarily in rural areas, be sure to run up hills, through brush and practice hurdling small objects such as rocks. If you work primarily in an urban setting, be sure to do some running on concrete, around people on crowded streets, or up flights of stairs. Routines might include stretching, reaching, rolling, and other exercises that strengthen your core muscles, as this conditioning will allow maximal execution of skills on the streets and in the field.

Substance Use and Abuse

We hope it is not necessary to emphasize the problems with substance use by prehospital personnel. However, it may be more necessary to do so when it is recognized and admitted that 1) alcohol is also an abused substance and 2) substances "only used to improve performance" may still be abused. Unfortunately we often "go easy" or want to overlook or rationalize drug use with a faulty belief that it is somehow different from street or recreational use when it is used for "performance enhancement."

There is reason to be concerned that substance abuse among pre-hospital emergency care providers is a problem, may be increasing, and that high risk substance use increases after traumatic events (McIntosh, 2007; Donnely & Siebert, 2009). Further, the emergency medicine literature periodically features research, such as Goldberg et al.'s work in 1996, which found levels of alcohol consumption to be a highly-ranked correlate of moderate to high burnout.

Volunteers make up a significant population of prehospital personnel, and it can be overwhelming at times for them to meet responsibilities of their family, their primary occupation, and their EMS responsibilities. Programs are available to assist pre-hospital personnel with life stress, incident stress and substance-related issues.

Amphetamine use to manage fatigue can be a problem. And the "less-lethal" form, caffeine, can be a problem, too. Caffeine certainly does not share the same stigma as alcohol or other abused drugs. However, everyone who uses caffeine soon recognizes that over time, tolerance comes into play. The standard cup of coffee does not carry the same "kick" after a while, and a larger or stronger cup is needed to have the same effect.

Energy drinks are becoming increasingly popular as well. Tolerance and addiction are not the only issues. Side effects can include increased anxiety, "being wired," impulsive acts, increased need to urinate, cardiac effects, and withdrawal during a prolonged call if there is no access to caffeine. These caffeinated beverages are certainly addictive and can still be abused.

We do not need a detailed discussion of all of the statistics and issues that surround performance-enhancing or mood-altering non-prescription medications. However, it is important to know that it is possible to enhance performance in ways other than by chemical use or abuse. Performance enhancement is the focus of this book, aimed at teaching psychological techniques you can also use instead of chemicals to do a better job.

Take Action

If you are going to use caffeine, try planning and managing your use of it. By doing so, you can increase the effects you get from it. Use it sparingly, and make it work for you. Assuming no medical contraindications, for instance, during a stretch of day shifts, have a cup of coffee in the morning, and if necessary, have a soda with lunch. If you have to switch to evening or night shift, have another soda when your energy starts to decline. Overall, less is better, so the caffeine will have an effect when you need it. We are not suggesting caffeine use or a specific manner of use, but rather to consider wisely planning and managing your use, if you choose to use caffeine. The best approach, though, is to be physically fit and to be well-rested.

Sleep and Sleep Deprivation

If you sell yourself short on sleep, your body, your main piece of equipment, is going to fail. It is clear from experience and research in both medical and nonmedical settings that excessive fatigue and sleep deprivation can have deleterious effects on performance, such as:

- slowed decision-making
- decreased motivation
- depressed mood
- slowed and inaccurate cognitive processing
- decreased ability to learn new skills

Indeed, one famous Cornell University sleep researcher summarized the research on sleep deprivation by saying that depriving the brain of sleep "makes you clumsy, stupid, and unhealthy." Shift work does not necessarily lend itself to good sleep patterns, and many other commitments demand our time when medical responsibilities do not. Consider your sleep habits and how they can be improved.

Take Action

Don't blow off your need for sleep. Make sleep a priority; recognize its importance to both your health and performance. Define and try to maintain a functional sleep pattern. However, if you are sleepy there are some things you can try to enhance alertness for a short period until you can get sleep.

To increase alertness on the job when you are fatigued, try to take a nap, but keep it shorter than 45 minutes. If napping is not an option, pay attention to your posture. Standing may combat fatigue better than sitting or reclining. Cool temperatures, bright lighting, and doing a variety of tasks can help sustain alertness. Chewing gum has also been shown to aid in fighting fatigue.

From physical conditioning to enhanced nutrition to guarding sleep and down-time, focus on, and don't slight, the multiple physical approaches that will maximize your psychological performance as well.

Chapter 2

Mental Lights and Sirens:
Arousal and Performance

*They are subject to the stresses of life and the
effects of being exposed to excessive danger,
destruction and human misery.*

~Drs. Jeffrey Mitchell & Grady Bray

In an emergency situation, a fundamental requirement
for optimal performance is to understand and control
physiological arousal. This is related to the well-known
"fight or flight" response. (There is actually a third "F"
which is to freeze under stress). Adrenaline and other
stress chemicals released in the body during high-stress
situations impact how you respond to these situations.

Arousal can be physical or psychological—and is
usually both. How you understand and manage arousal
dictates how well you perform during an emergency
situation. There are two kinds of arousal: primary and
secondary. Primary arousal results from the performance
demands of the emergency situation. It should provide the
necessary preparatory readiness to respond by increasing
energy and enhancing alertness. Primary arousal facilitates
your actions during an emergency and helps you meet the
challenge before you.

Secondary arousal, however, results from aspects of the
emergency situation unrelated to meeting the challenge,
such as not feeling ready or prepared, worrying about how
you will justify your actions, being afraid of failure, or not
performing well in front of others like colleagues and
patients. Secondary arousal jeopardizes your performance
because its occurrence and intensity are unpredictable, it
is harder to control, and it tends to inhibit effective
performance.

There are two models of the relationship of arousal and quality of performance. The first is called Drive Theory and looks like this:

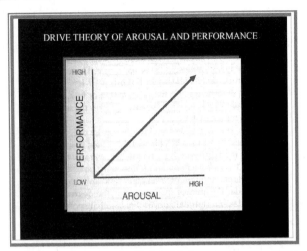

Drive Theory states that the higher your level of arousal, the better you perform. It suggests that more arousal is better and that arousal can never be too high.

The other model is called the Inverted U Theory or Upside-Down U Theory (or technically, the Yerkes-Dodson Law after the military researchers who first described it). It says that for any skill, task, or situation, there is an optimal level of arousal that leads to peak performance.

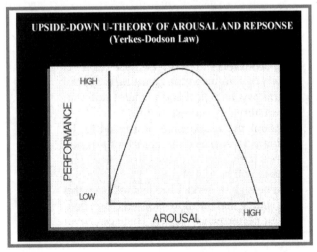

Too little arousal fails to make your skills sharp enough to perform well while too much arousal becomes distracting and impairs performance. While experience and research provide most support for the Inverted U Theory, the main point for you to remember is that arousal itself is not all bad. We need some degree of arousal to perform at our maximum capacity.

Learning how much arousal we need and how to target and control our levels of arousal is the key to optimizing performance during critical situations. Lima and colleagues (2002) measured stress by pulse and blood pressure in physicians undergoing ACLS training. They found that stress impacted these vital signs and lessened the effectiveness of the learning process and efficiency of emergency training.

Research with firefighters showed the difference between exercise and arousal due to emotion and how mental challenges can magnify stress responses beyond those with just physical demands. Webb et al. (2006) studied firefighters in two situations. One was exercising to 60% breathing capacity, a physical challenge, and the other situation involved exercising to 60% breathing capacity while simultaneously doing a computerized fire strategy and tactical drills decision challenge task, a combined physical and mental challenge.

The firefighters involved in the physical and mental challenge perceived the workload to be harder than that of the physical challenge group. With the addition of mental stress, there was an elevation of the firefighters' stress hormones: epinephrine/adrenaline, norepinephrine, and cortisol. The mental challenge of emergency care, which is central to what you do, can add significant stress during a response.

The Upside-Down U effects are not limited to physical skills. Essential to quality performance is situational awareness; you need to be cued-in to what is happening around you and what it means for the immediate future. Your level of arousal impacts your situational awareness. When there is too little arousal, you are not adequately alert. But too much arousal leads to overload and an inability to process information and act effectively. Siddle

15

(2009) emphasized the critical role of situational awareness, or precision in perception, during emergency medical situations.

Other factors impact the arousal-performance relationship. Individual characteristics and the nature and complexity of and experience with the skill or task affect performance.

Different skills or tasks require different levels of arousal to be performed in an optimal manner. Although critical skills, such as intubating patients and starting IVs, tend to generate high levels of arousal, they are typically performed better under lower levels of arousal. The complexity of the skill is another factor as to how arousal levels affect the quality of performance. Simple skills allow more arousal without compromising quality, but complex skills can deteriorate more easily with stress.

Related to this, an individual's experience must be considered in the relationship between arousal and performance. Well-practiced skills allow higher arousal levels without becoming impaired compared to new skills. This is the rationale for repetitive training in all kinds of situations, particularly high stress situations. When things go bad, you resort to your training and the neuromuscular connections that have been made, known as muscle memory. When that stressful event happens, and you feel the urge to fight, flee, or freeze, your training will get you through the event.

Finally, keep two things in mind. First, we are talking about physical and psychological reactions that come from *emotional* arousal, or emotional stress; not stress from sprinting 150 yards or up three flights of stairs.

Secondly, remember that the effect of arousal on performance varies by individual. Some medical personnel perform better with more arousal while others need to be as relaxed as possible to perform their best. While you may not be an "adrenaline junkie," you probably enjoy a fairly high level of arousal or you wouldn't be doing emergency work in the first place.

Nonetheless, it is important that you find your O-ZONE or Optimal Zone of Natural Excellence. This is the level of arousal where you perform your best; regardless of whether it is high, low, or somewhere in the middle. Find your optimal level of arousal, or optimal zone of natural excellence, to maximize your performance. Remember, feeling some arousal is a sign of readiness to respond and perform at your best.

The zone is also associated with "the flow experience," a state where everything seems to click and the effort seems flawless (Csikszentmihalyi, 1990). Flow experiences reflect the Inverted U curve. Goleman (1997) reports that flow is most likely to occur when someone finds a task he is skilled in and that slightly challenges his ability. Too little challenge leads to boredom while too much challenge leads to anxiety. Flow occurs in that "delicate zone between boredom and anxiety." Perry (2005) suggests that flow cannot be forced or directly created. It occurs when skills and abilities match the task.

The characteristics usually associated with flow experiences are described as (Gauron, 1984):

- Merging of action and awareness
  - thinking and doing flow as one; merging of self with task
- Focused attention
  - all that enters awareness is needed for success
  - awareness is filled with only relevant information
- Sense of control
  - feeling smooth control over self and environment
  - feeling confident, not invincible
- Sense of clear demands and direction
  - decisions seem easy
  - clear direction
- Inherent satisfaction

While the adrenaline-related arousal under stress has life-saving and performance-enhancing effects, it can also degrade performance. Learning to recognize your best levels of arousal and your optimal performance state (O-ZONE) and then using the techniques discussed throughout this book to achieve them can help maximize your performance.

Define your O-ZONE. Think about your most successful medical emergency experiences. These are the experiences where you were in the zone and on your game. On a scale of one to ten, where one represents being very relaxed and ten represents being very "revved up," how high was your arousal? Then think about the times when you did not perform the way you would have liked or things did not go well. How high was your arousal during these situations? You will likely start to see a pattern of what degree of arousal works best for you, your O-ZONE.

Another approach to defining your O-ZONE is to participate in multiple or repeat training simulations in which you respond after getting yourself into different levels of arousal: high, medium, or low. Try out different levels of arousal during training and then think: At what level did you feel most comfortable? At what level did you do your best? At what level was your thinking the clearest? Use your reactions and performance during training at these different levels of arousal to define your optimal zone for performance.

Chapter 3

Mental Alarms:
Stress, Fear, and Mental Toughness

I count him braver who overcomes his desires
than him who conquers his enemies,
for the hardest victory is victory over self.

~Aristotle

The challenge in a medical emergency is control:
control of the clinical situation, control of the emergency
response, and control of yourself. Typically, the goal is to
control or manage the excessive arousal that is often
innate to such actions. However, there are times when
under-arousal, or too little arousal, is the problem.

Under-Arousal

There are times when you need to increase your
arousal, such as being fatigued at the end of a busy shift,
being bored on an extended shift, feeling "not that into it,"
or being paged from a deep sleep. All of these situations
call for ways to increase performance arousal, such as
physical warm-ups; cue words; cue images; attentional
focus; self-efficacy statements; and music.

Take Action

The next time you are suffering from under-arousal on
shift, try some of the following suggestions:

19

1. Do some jumping jacks, toe raises or arm circles to stretch and increase your heart rate a little to help raise your level of arousal.
2. Come up with some *cue words*, like "focus, think, plan, react, ready, or now," etc. that can raise your level of arousal.
3. Imagine yourself responding well during an emergency situation. This kind of *cue image* is a powerful preparation and performance enhancement technique.
4. Consciously block out irrelevant thoughts and focus all of your energy on your response to the emergency situation. This type of *attentional focus* can be made easier by running a checklist of all of the tasks that need to be done in a given situation.
5. Tell yourself "I am feeling ready," or "I'm feeling good," or "I'm feeling sharp," etc. Such *self-efficacy statements* instill a powerful sense of confidence.
6. Listen to the *music*. Music is probably the main technique used by athletes to manage mood and energy while preparing to perform at maximum levels. You can develop a response-performance tape of music (slow, fast, or rockin') that helps create the level of arousal you need and puts you in your O-ZONE.

Once you have mastered any or all of these techniques, it is useful to share them with those on your team. Remember, no one responds in a vacuum; teamwork is key.

Response Stress

Response stress in medical emergencies can be defined as a *perceived imbalance between the demands of the emergency situation and your ability to meet those demands where failure to do so has important consequences to you.*

Every emergency situation has three aspects: (1) the **objective situation** refers to the nature of the medical emergency; (2) you make an **appraisal** of the situation and evaluate your ability to handle it; and (3) an **emotional**

response that has behavioral, psychological, and physical reactions that affect the quality of your performance.

When you feel prepared to act, your stress is minimal, you feel confident, and your arousal level is optimal. However, when you feel ill-prepared, your stress increases.

Perception plays a large role in how you handle a situation. Some individuals may feel unready to respond when they might actually be very capable. Others may feel confident when more caution is warranted.

This definition of medical emergency stress also points out that stress occurs only when you care about the outcome of your actions and the consequences of not succeeding. When the outcome matters most and you are invested in doing well, stress becomes very likely. If you do not care about the result, you will not feel stress (but usually this is not a reaction in those who provide emergency care).

The Institute of Medicine (2007) delineated some typical aspects of stress specific to emergency medicine. Patients are typically more acute and medically unstable than in other settings, and patient encounters are new and brief compared to "knowing" and following a patient in the office. Pre-hospital personnel also have to handle circadian shift issues, the severity of illness, the complexity of conditions, limited information, the unscheduled and uncontrolled nature of emergency calls, and high medico-legal risk. All of these factors combine to add complexity to any emergency situation.

As we mentioned earlier, adrenaline is a performance-enhancing and life-saving chemical our bodies secrete in high stress situations. However, this effect will only occur when the release of adrenaline has been trained and restrained. When the adrenaline "dump" is untrained and unrestrained, it can inhibit and even severely degrade functioning (failing to act/fight, but rather inappropriately fleeing or freezing).

The negative impact of stress in individuals who have not been trained in mental toughness skills can manifest itself in a variety of ways. There may be perceptual changes: tunnel vision may occur, leading to missing signs and symptoms; tunneled hearing can occur, leading to poor communication, missed commands or misunderstood information; time may seem to slow down or speed up. Hicks (2008) wrote that in emergency medical care, maintaining situational awareness is a core crisis resource management principle. Situational awareness is essential for functioning and safety of patient and provider alike.

Psychological effects, such as fear and/or freezing; slowed decision time; memory distortion that affects recall; concentration lapses; and decreased tolerance for discomfort, pain, and frustration, can also be the result of unrestrained stress.

Other effects can be seen in impulsive behaviors such as acting before fully assessing, or demonstrating a "rescue fever," such as rushing into dangerous or unstable situations. There can be a "tactical fixation," or failure to change strategy or care when needed.

There can even be a regression or a return to basic ingrained non-professional behaviors, such as yelling for help, rather than providing it, which present before training in effective emergency actions.

High-stress situations can have even more of an impact as their characteristics exaggerate the negative potential of stress even more. High stress situations are defined by unusual or unexpected circumstances; a demand for multiple actions under difficult conditions, like time pressure, heat, cold, or inclement weather; and a complex environment, meaning that diagnosis and etiology may be unclear, or the situation is dynamic where apparent diagnosis, or even environmental safety issues, are fluid, dynamic and changing. Acute high-stress situations may be outside of standard operating procedures. Finally, all this comes together in the requirement for smooth and effective application of skills to avoid dire consequences or tragedies.

This book is not about general stress, life stress, or cumulative stress. However, it is important to realize that ongoing levels of stress in your life can affect acute stress responses. High levels of chronic stress can accelerate stress reactions in high stress situations.

Grossman and Christensen (2004) wrote that under stress, "You don't rise to the occasion; you sink to your level of training." Therefore, training in both physical and psychological skills is essential to minimize stress effects during medical emergencies.

Take Action

1. Think about what happens to your body when you are in a stressful situation. Does your stomach get upset? Do your palms sweat? Do you have trouble concentrating? As you continue to read this book, begin to practice and integrate the self-regulation techniques described for managing stress into your training and response. With practice, you will develop better control over your body's reactions to stress.

2. Always remember to make sure the scene is safe before you jump in to patient care. Becoming a casualty yourself is not the way to help your patient. Maintain situational awareness; guard against impulsive "rescue fever" driven actions.

Fear

Fear is a topic that is not discussed as much as it should be. Solomon (1990) defines fear as an automatic emotional reaction to a perceived danger or threat characterized by a high state of arousal. Rachman (1990) raises the interesting point that it may not be possible to demonstrate courage without feeling fear. Courage is defined as feeling, but confronting or overcoming, fear.

Fear can be seen as the ultimate stress. It involves excessive arousal that can inhibit effective functioning. However, fear can function to produce a readiness to respond, and it can signal the need for caution in certain situations. Understanding and managing fear is the key.

There are different types of fear, and each type of fear has a different approach to mastery (Feigley, 1989). Some typical types of fear and ways to deal with them are described in the following section.

REALISTIC FEAR

Realistic fears may be related to specific skills or situations. Fear of the unknown is a common realistic fear. Such fears are often a sign that more training is needed to minimize the potential for pain, injury, or death. These fears tend to subside with experience, which builds confidence. Remember, more of the same training is not always better. A different approach may be needed, such as setting appropriate and achievable goals during training.

Performance-enhancing imagery can also be useful in creating confidence in dealing with unlikely, unforeseen, or unusual situations. "What-If" questions and gaming can be used to train and prepare for difficult situations *if* you define responses to those situations *before* they occur and practice those responses in imagery or reality. Don't just ask "what if," but answer with effective potential responses.

1. Language is important when dealing with "what-if" fears. It is useful to change the what-if proposition to a **when-then** statement to convey greater certainty and specificity. *What if my patient stops breathing on the way to the hospital* turns into *When a patient stops breathing on the way to the hospital, then I will intubate the patient.*
2. Simulation can be an extremely useful approach for fear of the unknown. Sometimes just having time to explore or be in fearful situations at one's own pace

can reduce uneasiness. If you do not fe
comfortable operating your rig's heart n
spend some time using it and experimen
of its capabilities in between calls instead
watching TV. You'll feel more comfortable a
control the next time you have to use it on a
patient.

3. Performance-enhancing imagery can also be useful
in preparing for the unknown by mentally
rehearsing responses for various situations.

ILLOGICAL FEAR

Illogical fear is fear that is out of proportion to objective
realities. It is often seen in self-doubts that are greater
than what they should be. Illogical fears result from a
distortion in perception of a situation. Comments, such as,
"I always mess up intubating patients," represent illogical
fears. Words, like "never" and "always," are usually
exaggerations, but they are so powerful that they create
fear.

Take Action

1. Try using self-talk (discussed in more detail in
chapter seven) the next time illogical fears creep
into your mind. Instead of saying, "I always mess
up intubating patients," tell yourself that you have
practiced your intubation skills a lot recently and
that you have the skills necessary to intubate
patients on the first attempt. Review how to
successfully intubate a patient by "talking yourself"
through the steps needed.

FEAR OF FAILURE

Fear of failure is a complicated fear that is common among highly motivated people. High motivation comes from two sources: The Motive to Achieve Success (MAS) and the Motive to Avoid Failure (MAF). MAS-driven people like challenges, like to solve problems, use setbacks as a way to drive them harder, like seeing the outcome of efforts, and like to try new things. MAF-driven people are driven because they fear and want to avoid the embarrassment of failing. While they can perform well, they perform under great stress, worry, and pressure and are devastated by setbacks. They strive for the relief of obtaining a successful outcome and being finished with their task. Pre-hospital personnel are a blend of MAS and MAF. Positive training, which emphasizes development and success, fosters MAS, while negative failure-based training fosters MAF.

Take Action

1. Always remember that mistakes are a part of learning and present an opportunity for improvement.
2. One's self-concept and self-worth must be separated from a single performance situation. Grossman (2004) stated, "Never judge yourself by your worst day."
3. Try learning skills in small, achievable steps to experience success. A positive training philosophy also helps to alleviate the fear of failure.

ANXIETY

Anxiety is an important common reaction that is related to fear. Fear occurs when there is uneasiness about a specific situation whereas anxiety is a diffuse uneasiness without specific focus. Anxiety can also be seen as arousal that has become too intense or occurs from the wrong sources.

Take Action

1. The nature of the anxiety should help suggest a solution. Progressive muscle relaxation, performance-enhancing breathing, or biofeedback can help manage anxiety.

FUN FEAR

Fun fear is found in thrill activities, like riding roller coasters. This is really more a state of arousal than fear, which people can enjoy. Many EMS workers label themselves "adrenaline junkies" because they like the arousal that emergency situations create. Control and mastery of the situation are the key elements of fun fear.

Managing Arousal, Stress, and Fear

Chief Kevin Nelson captured a philosophy of accepting and transforming fear by saying,

You replace fear of a situation with respect for its challenges.

Experience is the usual way adaptation to stress occurs. Individuals who are experienced with a given set of skills show a different pattern of arousal from those with less experience with the same skill set. However, gaining experience requires time, which can be a luxury.

Simulation and performance-enhancing imagery are excellent approaches to gaining experience and exposure to various types of emergency situations more quickly and *before* they occur. Repeated training can moderate arousal and strengthen emotional control. Unfortunately, time and access may limit training of this nature. However, using the psychological skills described in the following chapters adds another dimension to your training for performance excellence by developing an effective and necessary level of control of your emotions and responses to arousal.

Chapter 4

Mental Diazepam:
Arousal Control and Mental Toughness

The difference between towering and cowering is totally a matter of inner posture.

~Malcolm Forbes

Maximizing performance and preventing the performance degrading effects of stress involves controlling your arousal so that your O-ZONE can be achieved and maintained. This involves learning self-regulation techniques, or Arousal Control Techniques (ACTs), which are discussed in detail in this chapter. Techniques to up-regulate or increase arousal have already been discussed. Techniques to down-regulate or reduce excessive arousal from the adrenaline dump are also critical to maximal performance.

We can describe these approaches only briefly, as many of the ACTs require further education and training beyond that which can be presented in this book. However, it is valuable to be aware of these techniques, for they all have potential benefits. These techniques, as well as other concepts discussed in this book, can be pursued through discussions with psychologists or medical professionals who may be attached to your emergency service agency. Community programs such as the YMCA or YWCA, also often offer education and training in physical conditioning approaches and self-regulation techniques like meditation or yoga.

However, be certain that those from whom you seek guidance actually have expertise in applying techniques to performance enhancement in general and to emergency care situations, in particular, and not just clinical problems.

29

The Relaxation Response

Dr. Herbert Benson developed this "Americanized" meditation technique in 1975 at the Mind-Body Institute and Harvard Medical School. The technique involves sitting comfortably in a quiet place and repeating a word or phrase that suggests relaxation to you. This is a passive method of inducing relaxation, meaning that it is important to focus on the word or phrase to let the relaxation happen. You cannot force it. Relaxation involves "letting go" to allow a calmer state to evolve.

Meditation and Yoga

These are ancient Eastern techniques that are very effective ways to control and quiet the body. You can slow down your pulse and breathing, lower your blood pressure, slow your metabolism and diminish muscle tightness by practicing meditation and yoga. Meditation is based on concentrating on or chanting a word or phrase while yoga is based on rhythmic breathing techniques in conjunction with dynamic body postures. Some research suggests that several forms of meditation can improve concentration, reaction time, learning, and memory (Walsh and Shapiro, 2006).

Self-Hypnosis

This technique is a form of concentration control where focus on one object or thought is so strong that everything else seems to be blocked out. For example, if we ask you how your shoes feel on your feet, you could tell us if they are comfortable or not. Prior to asking you, though, you probably were not aware of your shoes at all. This lack of conscious awareness of your feet (until directed to be aware) is a form of self-hypnosis. Daydreaming is another example of a spontaneous self-hypnotic state. Rather than have this happen by chance, you can develop this as a skill.

Autogenic Training

This technique uses self-suggestions of warmth and heaviness in your body to induce relaxation.

Biofeedback

This technique incorporates any relaxation technique but informs you via a biofeedback instrument, such as a heart rate monitor or skin temperature sensor, if your body is actually responding and relaxing. The feedback allows you to refine and gain greater control over your body's responses to stress.

Progressive Muscle Relaxation

This technique is a physically and mentally active approach. It provides a good point of focus and has been shown to be superior to other relaxation techniques. It begins with tensing up and then relaxing different muscle groups in the body. Once mastered, you move on to the next level, called "letting go." This involves relaxing without tensing the muscles first; you simply "let go" of the tension.

Progressive Muscle Relaxation (PMR) works because tensing and relaxing muscles trains them to relax and release tension. When muscles relax, other parts of the body respond, too. Heart rate slows, blood pressure decreases, and breathing becomes slower and easier.

Training in PMR helps prehospital personnel to recognize signs of tension in their muscles. Initiating relaxation at the earliest signs of muscle tension makes it easier to reverse it, thereby improving performance. The process of psychological conditioning allows PMR to work fast, sometimes within seconds. This involves associating muscle relaxation with a cue word that you say or think to yourself, such as "focus," "smooth," "easy," or "relax." Focusing on the cue word and relaxing your mind and body creates an association between that cue word and controlled relaxation in your body.

Relaxation Imagery

This technique involves imagining a pleasant scene, which provides you with relaxing stimuli and blocks out negative or stressful images. While people often joke about "going to their happy place," your body will respond to images you create in your mind.

Performance-Enhancing Breathing (PEB) Techniques

PEB is quite useful in managing the arousal or stress of an emergency. Slow rhythmic breathing shifts the body into a more relaxed state. In fact, Siddle (1995) commented that "breath control should be a mandatory component of survival stress management."

Diaphragmatic breathing is a particularly effective technique for arousal control. It involves breathing anchored at your diaphragm, or "belly breathing." PEB techniques are effective because they counteract the effects of disrupted breathing that occurs under stress.

The goal is not to use diaphragmatic breathing all the time. Rather, when you notice tension starting to build, take one or two PEBs to back the tension down. Or, during a response, take one or two PEBs at various times to "reset" your levels of tension and remind you to stay in your O-ZONE. Finally, if a mistake or something that is distracting occurs, taking one or two PEBs is a good way to regain your focus.

1. Count to three and then take a breath as quickly as you can. Hold it for 2 seconds and then go back to breathing normally. Did you notice how when you did this, your breathing was not very deep? Did you

notice how your chest and shoulders tensed up like they do when you are stressed? You did not feel nearly as relaxed as you are likely to feel when you practice and master diaphragmatic breathing!

2. Now, place your hand, palm-down, on your stomach and your other hand, palm-down, on your chest. If you are breathing with your chest, which is less effective, you will see the hand on your chest rise and fall.

3. Now breathe deeply and low from your diaphragm. Notice how your stomach distends and how the hand on your stomach rises and falls. This is diaphragmatic breathing.

4. Purse your lips together, like you are breathing through a straw. This helps produce diaphragmatic breathing. Taking "little sips of air" may help induce diaphragmatic breathing, as well.

5. The next time you are in an emergency situation, take one or two diaphragmatic or other relaxation breaths to help break the cycle of increased stress.

Centering

Performance expert Dr. Robert Nideffer (1975, 1978) described a technique from the martial art of Aikido called "Centering" that is helpful in managing the stress of high-risk situations. The purpose of centering is to develop a controlled state of relaxed focus, which, to use the Japanese simile, is a "mind like still water."

1. Inhale slowly and deeply as you do when you take a diaphragmatic breath. Exhale and slowly let your eyes close as you imagine a leaf or feather floating

gently and slowly down, lower and lower until it comes to rest, floating softly at about waist-height. Then open your eyes and return to your regular breathing and activity. You can repeat this once or twice if needed. Please note that, initially, you should try centering in a safe and quiet environment. However, like PMR, you will eventually develop the skill to do it quickly, with your eyes open, in any position, focused but aware, even when you are in a chaotic situation. Remember to give yourself a command to refocus after centering.

Attention Control Training (ACT)

Dr. Nideffer also extended centering into a technique called Attention Control Training (ACT). This method of regaining focus is especially useful when an unexpected event occurs that distracts you, your stress level reaches an uncomfortable level, or when you cannot get over a mistake that you made.

1. Complete the centering process: inhale and exhale with your centering image. Then give yourself a cue, a clinically relevant instruction, to refocus on what you need to do. A cue could be "assess airway" or "review rhythm on the heart monitor."

Visuo-Motor Behavior Rehearsal (VMBR)

Suinn (1984) developed this technique, which combines relaxation and imagery techniques. By moving back and forth between a state of relaxation and imagery of performance in a response situation, feelings of control, relaxation, and confidence are psychologically conditioned.

However, this technique requires an expert trainer and must be done initially in a structured manner so that the user learns how to switch off the relaxed state and transition into performance imagery smoothly. This process is alternated until the individual can go through the phases alone and quickly to prepare for an emergency. Asken (1993) successfully applied VMBR to firefighting.

Stress Inoculation Training (SIT)

This method is a multi-faceted approach to mastering stress in difficult situations (Meichenbaum, 1976). SIT builds resistance to specific stressful situations and integrates well with simulation exercises. The initial stress inoculation training requires a psychologist skilled in this technique.

There are three phases to SIT: *cognitive preparation,* during which the rationale of SIT is presented and the stressful situation is analyzed; *skill acquisition and rehearsal,* during which arousal control skills are learned and practiced; and *application,* during which skills are implemented. Application of SIT for managing a stressful situation successfully involves four steps: preparation for provocation, engaging impact and confrontation, activating coping and managing arousal, and review and adjustment of how the process went.

These skills underscore why it is so important to understand the performance effects of stress. Without this knowledge to serve as a foundation for training, pre-hospital personnel may become distracted and may not fully understand what happens to them under stress.

They may have "heard things" about how they should or should not respond psychologically in a high-stress situation and then become upset if they do not respond similarly. By understanding stress effects on performance and mastering ACTs, pre-hospital personnel gain greater flexibility in dealing with intense situations.

Your objective in self-regulation is to gain control over the physiology of stress. Remember, though, that mastering any of the various forms of relaxation takes practice, and you have to be smart about when to use them. You want to be in your O-ZONE during an emergency, not overly relaxed! Always practice in a safe environment. Also, keep in mind that if you have a health concern, especially post-traumatic stress disorder (PTSD), you should check with your doctor before pursuing techniques like relaxation training or imagery.

Chapter 5

Mental Scans:
Performance-Enhancing Imagery and Mental Toughness

Limits begin where vision ends.

~Gary Mack, *Mind Gym*

Performance-Enhancing Imagery (PEI), also known as mental rehearsal, is a natural process that can be one of the most powerful psychological skills for managing stress and enhancing performance in emergency medical situations. We all frequently engage in mental rehearsal or imagery when we anticipate our involvement in any situation, including patient encounters or what lies ahead of you during your shift.

Remsberg (1986) may have been one of the first to discuss imagery in high-stress situations. He called it "crisis rehearsal," which was a good idea, but was not the best term because it is the response and your performance that should be the focus of imagery training, not the crisis. Imagery is widely used in competitive sport (Morris, Spittle & Watt, 2005), but has also been recognized as being useful in maximizing emergency response skills (Asken, 1993), hospital emergency skills (Asken & Nystrom, 2009), and military and police skills (Murray, 2004; Asken, 2005; Asken and Grossman, 2010).

Imagery practice has been classically defined as the symbolic rehearsal of a motor skill in the absence of any gross muscular movement (Richardson, 1969). Performance-enhancing imagery is the use of your imagination to improve performance and the specific skills needed in emergency medical situations. Consider PEI as the mental rehearsal of skills or situations.

PEI can be used to enhance performance in many ways. For instance, it can be used to improve cognitive and motor skills. It can complement and enhance specific emergency

37

response skills, such as assessment and establishing an airway, and even improve personal and team interaction skills. It provides another round of practice of cognitive and motor skills even when reality-based simulations are not available. Hall (2002) suggested that PEI can be especially useful in the early stages of learning a new technique and can help reduce time needed to master that particular technique. He also reported that not engaging in imagery may impair learning of a simple motor task.

PEI can help analyze and correct mistakes, simulate situations, prepare you for specific situations, gain "experience," maintain skills, and enhance confidence.

Mental imagery can be particularly useful in skills that are sequenced, such as ACLS skills. By imagining the details of the algorithm, you not only "practice" the procedures, but you can also check for any points of uncertainty or confusion about the appropriate next step. If you cannot complete the procedure smoothly using imagery, you probably cannot execute it effectively in reality.

Hall (2002) also described how PEI can help maintain skills. Lammers et al. (2008) stated that procedural skill decay, or the loss of some or all of the component skills necessary to perform a procedure after a period of non-use, has been well-established in medical training. CPR skills or airway management skills can degrade in as little as weeks to 14 months. Imagery is used to keep skills fresh (Murphy, 2005). Murray (2004) states, "even when you don't have the resources to actually practice a skill, positive mental imagery is a tool that those who are at the top of their game use to maintain and improve proficiency."

What is particularly important here is that there are ways to make imagery maximally effective. For instance, image using all of your senses, not just what you "see" during a response. This more realistically mimics real-life situations that always involve all of your senses. While you often hear the term "visualization" used for PEI, we don't like this term because it suggests that you only think about what you see in an emergency—when in reality all of your senses are engaged and need to be imaged to maximize performance.

Use the "best perspective" when doing your imagery. There are two major perspectives: *external/third person* and *internal/first person*. The external/third person perspective is when your imagery is like the experience of observing yourself on video or from a spectator's view. The internal/first person perspective is comprised of imagery of seeing and experiencing what you do when you are actually in the situation (you see the patient in front of you, hear the radio, etc.) While our experience and preference is for responders to try to image in the first person/internal perspective (as this is most like the reality of a response), there is no real strong evidence to suggest that this perspective is more effective. So you can use either perspective, or both!

Effectiveness is increased when you image skills and actions carefully, correctly, and in real-time. Just like physical practice, incorrect, sloppy, or lazy effort translates into poor performance in the real world.

Make your images as vivid as possible. You can use partial movements and pantomime the skills to enhance the effect of imagery. You don't have to sit still while you do your imagery.

Finally, remember to image problems or unexpected occurrences during a response; *always* follow-up with imagery of how you will handle the problem or unexpected occurrence when it happens. Negative imagery has a negative impact on the quality of your performance, so while there should be preparation for handling unanticipated and critical situations, never stop with the problem image; always go to a successful image of how that problem will be handled.

PEI is an effective and safe technique. However, there are some cautions associated with the use of imagery (Morris et al., 2005, Murphy, 2005). First, PEI is not a substitute for physical practice. Next, people have varying abilities to image. Don't be upset or conclude you will not perform well in an emergency if you are not a strong imager. Often, the ability to image can be improved as a skill with practice.

Effective PEI requires some level of familiarity with the skill or response through physical training, practice, and experience. It is unlikely that realistic images of a skill or other emergency responses can be fully developed without having had some engagement with actual situations first. This is imagery of performance skills, not fantasy.

It is possible that imagery can cause anxiety, although this is usually a result of spontaneous negative imagery related to worry or from untrained or inadequate imagery. In addition, undisciplined imagery could be distracting, such as when you think about your dinner plans instead of engaging in the emergency situation. Again, such distraction usually occurs due to inadequate practice.

Another caution is that, while the occurrence is very rare, PEI can lead to overconfidence. Ramsey et al. (2006) noted that using imagery may result in feelings of confidence about performance that exceed actual ability, or "imagination inflation." PEI is to be integrated with intensive and consistent comprehensive training.

Finally, remember that imagery should be used with caution and guidance in individuals with a history of PTSD or other emotional issues.

To review, remember these key points about PEI:

1. There are many effective applications.
2. It is not a substitute for scenario or other skills training.
3. The key is to simultaneously integrate live training with imagery training.
4. Effective PEI requires some level of experience with the skill.
5. Using imagery within the context of trained psychological skills should actually reinforce the practice of all skills.

Take Action

1. Sit in a comfortable chair, relax, and close your eyes. Have someone read the following instructions to you:

   a. In your mind's eye, SEE an injured patient on scene.
   b. In your mind's ear, HEAR the commotion of others' actions, the family telling you what happened to the patient.
   c. In your mind's touch, FEEL the back board as you help lift the patient.
   d. In your mind's emotion, EXPERIENCE a sense of confidence as you interact effectively with your team and the patient and provide effective emergency care. Experience the sense of satisfaction as the patient is stabilized.
   e. In your mind's olfaction, SMELL the blood from the patient's multiple lacerations.
   f. In your mind's gustation, TASTE a cool soda on your parched and hoarse throat after you successfully conclude your care.
   g. Close your eyes and feel good and refreshed; confident in building your mental toughness and psychological performance skills.

2. For each instruction, image the scene for a few moments, then open your eyes, clear your thoughts, and move on to the next scene. Make each image as vivid as possible, maintain your focus, and try not to let other thoughts distract you.

3. This gives you an idea of how to use PEI with all of your senses. Substitute other situations related to

your particular responsibilities as a way to practice and enhance imagery beyond just the visual.

As cautioned with the relaxation techniques described before, if you have a history of trauma or mental health problems, it is best if you undertake imagery training with the guidance of a professional.

Chapter 6

Mental Scopes:
Concentration Skills and Mental Toughness

Simply stated, the most critical factor in high level performance is attention to the right thing at the right time.

~Janelle & Hatfield (2008)

The ability to concentrate or focus is the most intuitively recognized, essential skill for responding effectively in a high-stress environment like an emergency medical situation. Performance expert, Dr. Robert Nideffer (1978), says about concentration and attention:

It's the ability to control attention under pressure and in response to changing demands that separates the average person from the super performer.

Gawande (2002) suggests that mistakes in medicine are not aberrant, nor are they necessarily committed by "bad doctors" or responders. Among multiple factors that raise the risk of a mistake is inattention, which can be increased by other contributing factors, such as haste and fatigue. To paraphrase him, *the cogent question is not how to keep bad responders from harming patients; it is how to keep good responders from harming patients.*

At any given moment, your five senses take in millions of pieces of information (Wilson, 2002), while your ability to process and attend to relevant information is much more limited, but obviously crucial. There is the need to effectively focus and sort relevant information without being distracted by the irrelevant.

This comes into play while responding in an emergency medical situation. You may see and hear all kinds of information, much of which may not be pertinent to your patient, diagnosis and needed action. Being able to pick out the details that do matter is crucial to making sure your patient has an optimal outcome.

Stress can degrade cognition in many ways. Murray (2004) described the work on the "Jangle Effect," which says that stress creates difficulty with some forms of reasoning, especially verbal problem solving, known as internal dialogue. Unfortunately, it is the internal dialogue, thinking and talking to ourselves, that we use to analyze and solve problems. As another effect, Staal et al. (2008) reported that stress shifts attention to the "here and now" and may degrade memory.

Kavanaugh (2005) summarized considerable research that shows stress can produce a variety of negative effects on cognition. Stress can lead to a reduced ability to analyze complex situations and to manipulate data, thereby oversimplifying assumptions and requiring more time to reach a solution. Also, stress can prompt you to make decisions based on incomplete information or worse yet, to fail to consider a range of alternatives. Finally, stress makes it easy to ignore long-term consequences of proposed solutions.

Group Think

Teamwork and high performance teams are becoming more and more a part of health care delivery (Jain, 2007), and especially in the emergency department and other emergency situations. The quality of teamwork determines outcomes (Salas et al, 2008), and the integration of individual performance remains an important factor in the quality of team function and success (Fernandez et al., 2008).

Of particular importance in emergency care at the team level is the phenomenon of stress-based "Group Think" (first discussed by Janis, 1973, and later by Kavanagh, 2005, Strentz, 2006). Group Think is a distortion of the creative potential for group problem solving that occurs when stress is not managed; it is the group form of what happens to individual thinking and cognition under stress. It can lead to poor outcomes.

The characteristics of Group Think include:

- An illusion of invincibility creating excessive optimism leading to extreme risks
- Unquestioned belief in the group's morality and ability
- Stereotyped views of the challenge and underestimation of the threat
- Group members ignoring important information
- Direct pressure on members to conform, especially those who express a counterview

Stress can also affect cognition by mental "stalls" where cognitive processes fail at one or more of several points. Disruption can occur at various phases of your response actions, including:

- Perception - you're not paying attention or you don't see the problem.
- Analysis/Evaluation - you cannot identify the problem or you misinterpret its significance.
- Strategy Formulation - your decision-making is absent or disrupted by stress.
- Motor Initiation - stress causes you to "freeze" or slows your actions.

Concentration is the ability to direct and maintain your thoughts and attention. The ability to concentrate is not automatic; concentration needs to be trained. It takes a great deal of energy to concentrate, and it can be quite tiring to maintain the degree of concentration that the situation demands. Recognize that "daily use" does not create the type of intense concentration needed in emergency medical situations.

Often, there is a mismatch between the degree of concentration needed in a situation and one's ability to engage in it. Wegner (1989) quoted the famous educator, John Dewey, to reinforce the need to sharpen our ability to concentrate:

We can't just wish our minds to go in one direction or another, to concentrate or suppress, without the necessary practice, know-how, and skill.

Excellence in concentration is a requirement for safe and successful action in emergency medical situations because suboptimal concentration leads to suboptimal performance and poor outcomes. Perry (2005) noted that once a skill is well-learned, or automated, it requires less conscious attention. However, pressure can shift attention away from relevant information or cues and can interfere with learned behavior. This is when "choking" can occur. Pressure also promotes perceptive tunneling, which limits our awareness and can lead to missing important signs, symptoms, or information.

There are some aspects to concentration and attention that are important to understand in order to maximize your response in high-stress situations. A critical parameter, alluded to above, is the breadth of concentration or awareness. Attention can be broad and have a wide perspective, or it can have a narrow and tight focus. Just as with arousal, different tasks require different breadths of attention. Running a code or managing multiple patients requires a broad perspective while starting an IV and doing chest compressions demands a narrow focus.

Keep in mind that in medical emergencies, many situations require the ability to shift attention from broad to narrow or narrow to broad and then back again. Stress can inhibit functional attention, but with arousal control, performance is enhanced when there is a match between the breadth of concentration and the requirements of the situation.

Attention and Intention

Sonnon (2001) addressed the difference between "attention" and "intention." Attention refers to a broad focus, such as assessing or understanding a situation. Intention relates to a directed focus to engage in a specific act or to execute a specific skill. Sonnon cautioned about mixing the two, and he warned about excessive intention. While intention produces a focus on executing the skill, it can be so narrow that there is loss of awareness of other important signs, symptoms, or information present. Remember, during a medical emergency, it is important to pay attention to what is happening with the entire patient, not just to a particular task, such as starting the patient's IV.

As with the discussion about arousal and quality of performance, the point is to begin to think about what type of attention you need for different skills and tasks during a medical emergency. You need to consider duration, intensity, and flexibility by asking yourself if you can concentrate long enough (adequate duration), intensely enough (adequate intensity) and shift attention as needed (adequate flexibility). If you cannot answer positively to each of these questions, it would be of value to you to enhance your concentration and attention skills. This is essential, not only for excelling in your performance, but also for avoiding mistakes in performance.

Enhancing Attention and Concentration

There are a variety of ways to attempt to increase the effectiveness of concentration. As a basis, Perry (2005) reported that gaining an optimal level of arousal led to optimal attention skills. Actual training techniques for enhanced concentration range from simple exercises to rather involved computer-driven training. Computer games have been shown to maximize attention and focus when comprised of relevant content.

Take Action

1. **Attention-Fixation Training** is an accessible technique used to train concentration. It initially

involves sitting in a quiet place and choosing a "duty-related" object, such as a stethoscope, on which to concentrate. The idea is to learn to focus solely on the stethoscope and nothing else. You can develop increased focus in this manner:

- Focus on your stethoscope and nothing else for about 15 seconds. Notice its color, shine, scuff marks, scratches, anything about it and only it. If you become distracted by other thoughts (which suggests slipping mental discipline), bring your focus back on the stethoscope. When you are able to focus intently on your scope without distraction for 15 seconds, slowly increase your concentration time in increments of 15 seconds up to two minutes.
- Once you have achieved a concentration goal of two minutes, begin to introduce distractions, such as music or 'talk' radio. See if you can still focus solely on your stethoscope, being totally unaware if what is being said on the radio. Again, begin with a concentration period of about 15 seconds and try to work up to two minutes. You can also build resistance to distraction by turning up the volume after mastering a set period of concentration time.
- When you have gained some skill in your focus, alternate the distraction from narrow to broad; that is, move your attention from your stethoscope to the radio or what is going on in the room you are in. Then narrow your focus again to just your stethoscope. Remember, you want to train the ability focus and have flexibility in your focus; you don't want to train tunneled attention.
- It is also important and useful to train in the real world. Do some of these exercises in the ambulance or the station. Take a few minutes each day to practice focusing at the beginning of your shift.

2. **Conversation Concentration** is another technique to practice attentional focus. Whenever you find yourself in a social situation, especially if there is background conversation, you can practice shifting your focus. Move your attention from the person talking to you to conversations that are going on around you for brief periods. We often do this naturally, but we can use it to make attentional flexibility a more effective habit.

3. **Music**, or listening to music, can be used to train attention and focus. Try listening to your favorite music, but differently. Don't focus on the melody, words, or whatever you usually attend to; try to focus on the just the bass guitar, or just the drums, as a way to focus on a target stimulus while blocking out other distracting sounds. Again, be sure, at some point, to switch back and forth on your targets of concentration (the melody and background).

The above techniques can help strengthen attention, which is hard to maintain during a high-stress situation. These exercises can also improve attention flexibility and situational awareness.

Chapter 7

Mental Prescriptions:
STEP-UP

Self-Talk and Mental Toughness

Think like a man of action and act like a man of thought.

~Henri Bergson

Medical emergencies put cognitive skills to the test like no other situation. Emergency medical knowledge is critical, but what you think to yourself about your performance is central to how well you will apply your emergency skills. How and what medical responders think have a profound effect on their performance at all times, especially during high-stress situations.

Cognitive scientists have described important relationships among perception, cognition, and performance. This work and the performance applications of cognitive techniques have shown that our thoughts have a strong effect on our emotions and behavior, and, therefore, the quality of our performance.

Self-Talk

Most people experience thinking as "talking to themselves." This is called "self-talk," and it is a powerful process that affects your emotions, behavior and performance. Constructive self-talk is a powerful tool to maximize performance. In their work that focused on emergency team training strategies, Fernandez and her colleagues (2008) described the importance of teaching people to "think about thinking." Bond et al. (2008) stated that the goal of simulation training was to combine simulation with other strategies, like "thinking aloud," to review thought processes.

Performance expert, Dr. James Afremow of Arizona State University, labels the nature of self-talk as being either your internal enemy (negative self-talk) or your internal ally (positive self-talk). He asks, "What channel is your self-talk on?"

There are several important aspects to self-talk and its relationship to performance. For example, self-talk always occurs before you say anything, do anything, or feel any emotion. Self-talk is fast, and though you are often unaware of it, it is there. You can, however, become aware of your self-talk, and by doing so, you can change your self-talk, which can modify your response and performance. Finally, the more practiced a skill is, the quicker and "quieter" the self-talk becomes.

Duran, in *Developing the Survival Attitude* (1999), states, "You should understand that a relationship between words and actions does exist and that words can have a direct positive or negative impact . . ." As mentioned earlier in this book, preparation or training should focus on what to do "when" a situation occurs, not "if" a situation occurs.

This all becomes important when we consider the role of self-talk in the performance of daily responsibilities, and especially in high-stress situations. Your thinking and self-talk can be focused in one (or more) of four areas during a medical emergency. It can be focused on:

1. Content totally unrelated to the emergency situation, like what you would rather be doing or where you are going to eat later
2. Content related to the general nature of the emergency, such as the neighborhood where the call is occurring or what other emergency responders have shown up on the scene
3. Content related to encouragement, motivation or evaluation of efforts, such as telling yourself and your partner that you are prepared and are going to save the patient

4. Content related to specific decisions and actions that need you need to perform, such as deciding how and when to intubate the patient. This last category is known as *task-relevant instructional self-talk* (Asken, 1993) and is much like your instructor or mentor sitting on your shoulder and talking in your ear, coaching you through the steps and actions you need to take in the emergency situation.

If you think about it, you will understand that of these four possible focus points for your self-talk, only task-relevant instructional self-talk will consistently enhance your performance, and therefore, your success. It is even more important than that of encouragement and motivational pep talks because, while encouragement may have an effect on motivating you to do a good job, it does not tell you *how* to do a good job. This may be especially important for pre-hospital personnel during emergency situations. You need to know, and guide yourself on what to *do* in the emergency, not just be motivated to help.

Gawande (2007) offers that medicine is a "team sport" that shares commonalities with sports with two exceptions. First, the outcome is measured in human health and lives. Second, there are no coaches available. Gawande states that we have "no one but ourselves to lift us through the struggles."

Although his statement is perhaps a bit exaggerated, his points illustrate the fact that the nature of self-talk becomes crucial to the quality of performance. You can be and are your own coach or mentor for your responses. Self-talk will maximize the effectiveness of your self-coaching or mentoring.

To develop and use task-relevant instructional self-talk, we suggest using the STEP-UP model. Being able to STEP-UP (**S**elf-**T**alk for **E**nhanced **P**erformance-**U**nder **P**ressure) is, as we described above, like having your instructor or mentor sitting on your shoulder to relay instructions on what to do at each given point. It is how he or she would talk you through the skills needed in an emergency, and how *YOU will now talk yourself through needed actions to succeed.*

This type of self-talk is often a series of short cues that do not contain all of the details of actions that might be taken, but they do allow you to keep a focus and cue the interventions that are needed. For example (these are just examples, as you should develop your own set of phrases or cues that work for you), STEP-UP for an unexpected cardiac arrest might be:

- Focus and evaluate the patient
- ABC's
- ACLS algorithm
- Call medical command with status update
- Repeat

Or, an example of STEP-UP for an animal bite might be:

- Assess for scene safety: is the animal secured?
- ABCs
- Protect the wound
- Assess vital signs
- Secondary survey: any other injuries?
- Reassurance and transport

In addition to providing specific direction on what to do in the emergency, STEPPING-UP and the use of task-related self-talk is important in that it also blocks negative self-talk. When things are not going well, it is easy to get into a negative thinking cycle, which is discussed later. For now, realize that negative self-talk gets in the way of performance, so avoid it. Remembering to STEP-UP can help you achieve this goal. There are several ways to train to STEP-UP more effectively.

Take Action

1. Relax so that you can attain your optimal performance state or O-ZONE
2. Encourage yourself and avoid negative self-talk if you make a mistake. What you are doing is incredibly important, difficult, and skilled work.
3. Encourage others, and beware of using excessive sarcasm or "gallows humor" as a coping mechanism. While common in emergency services, it can erode confidence and the team spirit, especially in high stress situations.
4. Monitor and change self-talk to promote performance.

You can help facilitate this process by using a self-monitoring chart like this:

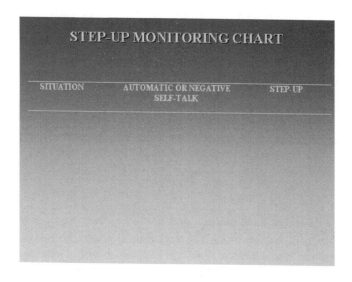

STEP-UP MONITORING CHART

SITUATION	AUTOMATIC OR NEGATIVE SELF-TALK	STEP-UP

It is important to look for situations where you might engage in automatic non-productive and/or negative self-talk. Write the situation and the "automatic" non-productive or negative self-talk in the first two columns. You might be able to do this by thinking about past situations where you became frustrated, upset, or stressed. Or, do it after a more recent encounter when memories and emotions are still fresh.

The crucial point is to then STEP-UP. Create and write in the third column (labeled STEP-UP) the words or phrases of your self-talk that will facilitate more effective performance.

The following chart illustrates an example of a potentially critical and stressful situation involving multiple trauma victims arriving at the emergency department on top of an already busy shift with critical patients. By recognizing and charting the automatic or negative self-talk that creates distraction and dysfunction, you can become aware of irrelevant thoughts, any negativity, and the source of further frustration. Also, note the STEP-UP response in creating more functional and task relevant self-talk to be used to replace the automatic or negative thoughts the next time a similar situation occurs.

STEP-UP MONITORING CHART

SITUATION	AUTOMATIC OR NEGATIVE SELF-TALK	SELF-TALK FOR ENHANCED PERFORMANCE (STEP-UP)
BUS TURNOVER WITH MULTIPLE CASULATIES	I CAN'T HANDLE THIS MANY KIDS	RAPID ASSESSMENT
	WE DON'T HAVE ENOUGH CREW	AIRWAY MANEUVER
	I'M NOT PREPARED FOR THIS	TRIAGE TAG
	WHAT IF I MISS SOMETHING ?	NEXT PATIENT
	WHAT IF SOMEONE DIES ?	

5. A final approach to maximizing self-talk for enhanced performance is to *always phrase your self-talk positively in terms of what you should do, not what you should not do.* Telling yourself not to do something puts the focus on what you want to avoid doing.

Why do we say this? For an answer, do this first. In the next two seconds, do not think of your ambulance. What did you just think of? Most likely: your ambulance. This is because of the six words in the statement, five of the six words (and the last four) tell you to think about the ambulance. Your mind doesn't separate that from the "not" in the sentence. Our brains are not built to *not think* of something. To not think of something, we have to first think of it! A better STEP-UP for not thinking about the ambulance would be to think of your service patch, or stethoscope, or toolbox, and so on.

So, phrase self-instructions in a positive way. For instance, say, "Stabilize the neck" instead of saying, "Don't move his neck." Telling yourself not to do something puts the focus on what you want to avoid doing. Remember, being aware of and managing self-talk can provide additional control for enhanced performance in high-stress situations.

Critical situations may not seem to allow time to "think" or to construct self-talk, especially since too lengthy or complicated thinking can get in the way of executing skills effectively. While there is some truth to this, it does not negate the impact of self-talk on performance. It really means that it is important for you to develop and practice how to STEP-UP prior to critical situations (as well as analyzing and learning from future experiences). Your self-talk should be short, response-oriented, focused, direct, and powerful enough to promote appropriate action and excellence.

The practice and training of integrating mental and physical skills promotes their merging together into a more automatic and seamless response. By planning and practicing, self-talk should become second nature, occurring automatically when needed. Indeed, whether you STEP-UP or your self-talk tears you down depends on your mental preparation and practice.

Chapter 8

Mental Ablations:
Negative Thought Stopping and Mental Toughness

They can conquer who believe they can.

~Virgil

There are many names for it: "Toxic Thinking,"
"Defeatist Attitude," or "Negative Thinking." Call it what
you want to, but one thing remains the same: this negative
cognitive state can easily degrade performance.
Understanding this process and, more importantly,
developing an effective intervention to "ablate" negative
thinking, is essential for maximizing performance.

Negative self-talk or negative thinking can interfere with
optimal performance in emergency medical situations in
many ways. It can degrade self-confidence because the
mind becomes programmed for self-doubt. Negative self-
talk can reduce concentration, making it difficult to focus
in a situation where focus is paramount to success.

Negative thinking and attitudes can spread to other
team members and to other aspects of your life. Negative
thinking is contagious; it easily spreads to others. Maxwell
(2001) calls this "The Law of the Bad Apple." We have all
been around "toxic" people who tend to bring out the worst
in us. Every conversation centers on negative things and
becomes a source of stress. It is best to limit contact with
such individuals because their negativity can easily spread
to other areas of your life, and negative self-talk can
become a destructive habit.

Martin (2006) said that members of Special Forces
hate to hear someone whining, not because the complaint
is not justified, but because they believe that that whining
means the person is not thinking about the right things to
be successful; focus and concentration are off, thereby

jeopardizing the success of the mission. Remember: think about what needs to be done to achieve a positive outcome.

Finally, negative thinking can create anxiety, stress, and depression. Indeed, Burns (1981) noted that the basis of cognitive therapy sees negative thoughts as instrumental in creating and maintaining anxiety and depression.

Expectations exert powerful influences on our behavior. Expectations flow from our thinking, self-talk, and, as we have been saying, the words we use. And, it is important to realize that negative expectations seem to be more influential on our behavior than positive ones. Consider that while telling yourself you will succeed at something may help motivation, success can not be guaranteed because there may be many other uncontrollable factors that affect the outcome. However, telling yourself that you *cannot* do something will surely guarantee failure or giving up.

As Thomas Jefferson pointed out:

Nothing can stop the man with the right mental attitude from achieving his goal; nothing on earth can help the man with the wrong attitude.

Negative thinking is at the root of self-doubt. The concept of a self-fulfilling prophecy says that our expectations about success or failure greatly influence our efforts and performance on a task. Henry Ford stated, "Whether you say 'I can' or 'I can't,' you are right."

Recent research seems to confirm this. It takes effort to overcome the "toxicity of negative affect," and a neutral problem-solving, task-relevant focus is needed for balance (Frederickson and Losada, 2006). Therefore, the key is to avoid negative thoughts. Stay neutral and problem-solving focused in your thinking and self-talk. Positive expectations can help motivation, and, when combined with the correct task-relevant instructional focus and self-talk, they can provide synergy to maximize performance.

However, it is likely that even with the best attempts to STEP-UP and to focus on task-relevant instructional self-talk, you will still have negative thoughts from time to time.

Therefore, a technique called Negative Thought Stopping (NTS) can be helpful in managing performance in high-stress situations. Developed by Dr. Joseph Cautela of Boston University, it is simple to implement and can be very effective.

In our training programs, we demonstrate NTS by asking participants to close their eyes and think about a negative or critical thought about themselves that is related to their performance or a recent stressful situation. After everyone has concentrated on that thought for about five seconds, the instructor suddenly bangs his hand on a table and yells as loudly as possible, "Stop it!" Everyone's eyes pop open as they sit bolt-upright and refocus their attention on the instructor.

At that point, when asked, usually every person acknowledges that the negative thought was (forcefully!) ejected from their minds. They are no longer thinking of it.

In an actual response situation, NTS occurs when the responder emphatically yells—internally to him or herself, and not out loud—**NO!** or **STOP IT!**, which over-rides and ejects the negative thought from their thinking. This is then followed by a self-command to return to focus on the medical challenge at hand. These refocusing commands might be "Back to it," "Assess," "Communicate," or "Respond," or the like. NTS effectively stops negative self-talk and returns your focus to positive actions.

Practice and develop your negative thought-stopping technique in this manner:

1. Monitor for the presence of negative thoughts.
2. If negative thoughts are present, yell forcefully to yourself, "NO!" or "STOP IT!" (Again, please note: yell to yourself, not out loud!)

3. Give yourself a task-oriented cue, such as "Focus" or "Back to it."
4. Continue to execute your skills for the task at hand. Some people imagine an actual stop sign or a flashing neon sign that says, "NO" instead of telling themselves to STOP. See which version works best for you.

Some people add performance imagery to enhance their actions, cue their behavior, and help refocus on the challenge at hand. For instance, after thinking, "NO," immediately think of a task-oriented cue, such as "CHECK VITALS," and then image yourself checking a pulse. This will cue you to resume treatment where you left off.

DISTRACTION, NOT SUPPRESSION

Wegner (1989) has contributed much to our understanding of what makes the control of thinking effective. He notes that just trying to "directly suppress" a thought is not effective. Remember, as discussed previously in this book, your mind is not designed to "not think of something."

In fact, trying to directly suppress a thought can cause you to focus on it even more; it can cause a "rebound effect," where you think about the banished thought even more frequently after you stop trying to suppress the thought; cause an "intrusive reaction," in which the thought recurs, bringing with it a strong emotional response that is usually negative; or it can cause a physiological response, usually negative stress-type reactions, such as increased blood pressure.

The use of distraction is much more effective than suppression. Distraction is thinking about something else or replacing the unwanted thought with one or more other thoughts. Most people use multiple thoughts as distracters, and this works well when the thoughts are of great interest and significance to you.

Take Action

1. The next time you are tired and uncomfortable, such as on-scene at an MVA in the middle of the night in the rain, instead of thinking about your discomfort (or trying to not think about your discomfort), focus on the task at hand; go through a checklist of actions taken and those that should be taken, remind yourself of the aid your are giving and the importance of what you are doing. Use the previously discussed techniques to self-regulate.

Considering and practicing NTS and distracting thoughts or self-statements prior to needing them in an emergency situation makes these techniques more effective at a critical moment. Try these techniques so that you can provide your patients with the best possible care in all situations.

Chapter 9

Mental Clinical Pathways:
Affirmations, Attitude and Mental Toughness

*What lies behind us and what lies before us are tiny
matters compared to what lies within us.*

~Oliver Wendell Holmes

Self-talk and NTS intersect in the concept of attitude.
They are the ingredients for creating and maintaining a
successful attitude. Maxwell (2001) captures its essential
role with the following passage:

Attitude is the advance man of our true selves.
Its roots are inward, but its fruit outward.
It is our best friend and our worst enemy.
It is more honest and more consistent than our words.
It is an outward look based on past experiences.
It is a thing that draws people to us or repels them.
It is never content until it is expressed.
It is the librarian of our past.
It is the speaker of our present.
It is the prophet of our future.

Attitude is the essence of success and survival in all
kinds of stressful situations. Hence, there is one other
approach to maximizing performance and attitude in
addition to self-talk and NTS that is worth briefly
discussing. This is the use of affirmations.

Ben Franklin wrote affirmations of his thirteen values
and carried them in his pocket watch. He had them with
him at all times and frequently reviewed them whenever he
checked the time (Andreas and Faulkner, 1994).

Affirmations are positive statements about ourselves
that we make to ourselves. They are truthful statements
about our abilities and motivations, not boasts that create
unrealistic expectations or hopes. They remind us of our

strengths, talents, skills, and goals. Affirmations work best when they are in the form of an "I" statement. They are most effective when they are stated in the present tense.

Examples of affirmations might be:

I am a dedicated and professional responder.

I strive to give every patient the best care I can.

I take pride in my attitude, actions and integrity.

Finally, affirmations should be reviewed, stated, or meditated upon daily. Andreas and Faulkner (1994) suggested that if an affirmation is not yet true, you can change the wording to promote its potential; "I can learn to be" can replace "I am."

There are three types of affirmations: personal, which are statements that recognize your unique qualities; professional, which are statements that recognize your distinct qualities as a health care provider; and performance, which are statements that highlight unique aspects of your skills and performance efforts. Affirmations and their related positive thinking can affect your motivation.

Take Action

1. Create your own set of affirmations, such as: "I am committed to excellence" or "In all duties and responsibilities, I take pride in my preparation"
2. Create a set of personal affirmations
3. Create a set of professional affirmations
4. Create a set of performance affirmations
5. Create a set of team affirmations
6. Review your affirmations on a regular basis

Remember, you can change your affirmations as your personal and professional development dictates. Some research suggests that affirmations can help reduce the physiological impact of a stressful situation, especially in individuals who may have less fully developed self-confidence (Sherman et al., 2009). Affirmations have also been shown to help change behavior (Armitage et al., 2011). You should use some caution when engaging in positive thinking, encouragement, or affirmations because while they can be effective techniques, they do not provide direction and focus on *how* to maximize performance in a specific high stress situation. (That's where STEPPING-UP is essential).

Perhaps the best source of effective attitude is your confidence in your ability to perform physically and psychologically, both of which can be enhanced by the techniques described in this book. With proper training, practice, and integration of the psychological skills discussed, you can bolster your quality of performance, confidence and motivation, pride and satisfaction.

References and Resources

Afremow, James (2008). Personal communication. Health and Sport Psychology Clinic, Arizona State University.

Andreas, S., & Faulkner, C. (1994). NLP: The New Technology of Achievement. New York: Harper

Armitage, C., Harris, P., & Arden, M. (2011). Evidence that self-affirmation reduces alcohol consumption: Randomized exploratory trial with a new brief means of self-affirming. Health Psychology, 30, (5),633-641.

Asken, M. (1993). PsycheResponse: Psychological Skills for Optimal Response by Emergency Responders. Englewood Cliffs, NJ: Brady-Prentice Hall.

Asken, M. (2005). MindSighting: Mental Toughness Skills for Police Officers in High Stress Situations. Camp Hill, PA. www.mindsighting.com.

Baubin, M., Schirmer, M., Nogler, M., et al. (1996). Rescuer's work capacity and duration of cardiopulmonary resuscitation. Resuscitation, 33, (2), 135-139.

Barrett, M. (2006). Cited in Repetition reverses med students' stethoscope shortcomings. Science Daily. January 18, www.sciencedaily.com.

Benson, H. (1975). The Relaxation Response. NewYork: Morrow.

Bond, W., Kuhn, G., Binstadt, E., et al. (2008). The use of simulation in the development of individual cognitive expertise in emergency medicine. Academic Emergency Medicine, 15, 1037-1045.

Burns, D. (1981). Feeling Good: The New Mood Therapy. New York: William Morrow.

Dingfelder, S. (2007). Your brain on video games. Monitor on Psychology, 38, (2), 20-21.

Di Nasio, J. (2006). The Law of Exercise Specificity: Is your workout real to help you in the field? www.policeone.com, 06-05-2006.

Donnelly, E., & Siebert, D. (2009). Occupational risk factors in the emergency medical services. Prehopsital and Disaster Medicine, 24, (5), 422-429.

Duran, P. (1999). Developing the Survival Attitude. NY: Looseleaf.

Ericsson, K. (2008). Deliberate practice and acquisition of expert performance: A general overview. Academic Emergency Medicine, 15, 988-994.

Feigley, D. (1989). Coping with fear in high-level gymnastics. Technique, Apr-June, 4-9.

Fernandez, R., Vozenilik, J., Hegarty, C. et al., (2008). Developing expert medical teams: Toward an evidenced-based approach. Academic Emergency Medicine, 15, 1025-1036.

Ferrell, M., Beach, R., Szeverneyi, N. (2006). An fMRI analysis of neural activity during perceived zone-state performance. Journal of Sport and Exercise Psychology, 28, 421-433.

Frederickson, B., & Losada, M. (2006). Positive affect and the complex dynamics of human flourishing. American Psychologist. 60 (7), 678-686.

Gauron, E. (1984). Mental Training for Peak Performance. Lansing, NY: Sport Science Assoc.

Gawande,A. (2007). Better: A Surgeon's Notes on Performance. NY: Picador

Goleman, D. (1997). Emotional Intelligence. New York: Bantam.

Goodspeed, R. & Lee, B. (2007). What If...?: A survival Guide for Physicians. Philadelphia: F.A. Davis.

Green, S., & Bavelier, D. (2006). Effect of action video games on the spatial distribution of visual attention. Journal of Experimental Psychology: Human perception and performance, 32,(6), 1465-1478.

Griffin, M, & Cooper, C. (2006). Using near-infrared spectroscopy to "measure" imagery. NASPSPA Abstracts 2006, Journal of Sport and Exercise Psychology, 28, 576-577.

Hall, J. (2002). Imagery practice and the development of surgical skills. The American Journal of Surgery, 184. 465-470.

Hendricks, M. (2000). Physician, writer, philosopher, sage. Johns Hopkins Magazine, 52, (2), 65.

Honig, A., & Sultan, S. (2004). Reactions and resilience under fire. What an officer can expect. The Police Chief, 71, (12), www.policechief.org.

Institute of Medicine (2007). Hospital-Based Emergency Care: At the Breaking Point. Washington, DC: national Academy of Sciences, National Academies Press.

Jain, A., Thompson, J., Chaudry, J., et al., (2008). High performance teams for current and future physician leaders. Journal of Surgical Education. www.sciencedirect.com, 11-14-2008.

Janelle, C., & Hatfield, B. (2008). Visual attention and brain processes that underlie expert performance: Implications for sport and military psychology. Military Psychology, 20 (Suppl. 1), S39-S69.

Janis, I. (1973). Victims of Groupthink: A Psychological Study of Foreign Policy Decisions and Fiascos. Boston: Houghton-Mifflin.

Kavanagh, J. (2005). Stress and Performance: A Review of the Literature and Its Applicability to the Military. Santa Monica, CA: Rand Corporation.

Koltnow, S. (2004). Physician well-being. In J. Tintanalli, G. Kalen, & J. Stapczynski. Emergency Medicine: A Comprehensive Study Guide. NY: McGraw-Hill.

Lammers,R., Davenport, M., Korley, F., et al., (2008). Teaching and assessing procedural skills using simulation: Metrics and Methodology. Academic Emergency Medicine, 15, 1079-1087.

Lima, E., Knopfholz, J., & Menini, C. (2002). Stress during ACLS courses: is it important for learning skills? Arq Bras Cardiology, 79, (6), 589-592.

Maxwell, J. (2001). The 17 Indisputable Laws of Teamwork. Nashville: Thomas Nelson.

Martin, J. (2006). Get Selected for Special Forces. Yuma, AZ: Warrior-Mentor Press.

McIntosh, A. (2007).Substance abuse rises among paramedics – California. EMS Network News. www.emsnetwork.org.

Meichenbaum, D. (1985). Stress Inoculation Training. Elmsford, NY: Pergamon Press.

Morris, T., Spittle, M., & Watt, A. (2005). Imagery In Sport. Champaign, Ill: Human Kinetics.

Murphy, S. (1996). The Achievement Zone. New York: Putnam.

Murphy, S. (2005). Imagery: Inner theater becomes reality. In S. Murphy (ed.) The Sport Psych Handbook. Champaign, Il: Human Kinetics.

Nideffer, R. (1985). Athlete's Guide to Mental Training. Champaign, Il: Human Kinetics.

Nideffer, R., & Sharpe, R. (1978). Attention Control Training: How to Get Control of Your Mind Through Total Concentration. New York: WideView Books.

Ochoa, F., Ramalle-Gomara, E., Lisa, V., et al. (1998). The effect of rescuer fatigue on the quality of chest compressions. Resuscitation, 37, (3), 149-152.

Perry, C. (2005). Concentration: Focus under pressure. In S. Murphy (Ed.). Sport Psych Handbook. Champaign, Il: Human Kinetics.

Rachman, S. (1990). Fear and Courage. NY: WH Freeman.

Sanders, C., Sadoski, M., van Walsum, K, et al., (2008). Learning basic surgical skills with mental imagery: Using the simulation centre in the mind. Medical Eucation, 42, (6), 607-612.

Semeraro, F., Signore, L., & Cerchiari, E., (2005). Retention of CPR performance in anaesthetists. Resuscitation, Nov.

Sherman, D., Bunyan, D., Cresswell, J., & Jaremka, L. (2009). Psychological vulnerability and stress: The effects of self-affirmations on sympathetic nervous system response to Naturalistic stressor. Health Psychology, 28, (5), 554-562.

Siddle. B. (2009). The stress paradox. The War on Trauma: Lessons Learned From a Decade of Conflict. Supplement to the Journal of Emergency Medical Services, October, 2008, 28-31.

Sonnon, S. (2001). Keeping the Edge: Flow State Performance Spiral. Atlanta, GA: AARMACS.

Soohoo, S., Takemoto, K., & McCullagh, P. (2004). A comparison of modeling and imagery on the performance of a motor skill. Journal of Sport Behavior, 27, (4), 349-366.

Staal, M., Bolton, A., Yarowish, R. et al., (2008). Cognitive performance and resilience to stress. In Lukey, B., & Tepe, V. (eds.) Biobehavioral Resilience to Stress. Boca Raton, FL: CRC Press.

Starr, L. (1987). Stress inoculation training applied to cardiopulmonary resuscitation. Paper presented at the 95th Annual Meeting of the American Psychological Association, New York, New York.

Strentz, T. (2006). Psychological Aspects of Crisis Negotiation. Boca Raton, FL: CRC.

Wang, E., Quinones, J., Fitch, M., et al., (2008). Developing technical expertise in emergency medicine –the role of simulation in procedural skill acquisition. Academic Emergency Medicine, 15, 1046-1057.

Wegner, D. (1989). White Bears and Other Unwanted Thoughts. New York: Penguin.

Wilson, T. (2002). Strangers to Ourselves: Discovering the Adaptive Unconscious. Cambridge, MA: Belknap Press of Harvard University.

PHOTO CREDITS:

HaywireMedia/ Dreamstime.com

ABOUT THE AUTHORS

KERRY ANNE WHITELOCK, D.O.

Kerry Anne Whitelock, D.O. received her Honors degree in biology, a minor in world literature, and a master's degree in nutrition, all from The Pennsylvania State University-University Park Campus. During this time, she also served as a volunteer Emergency Medical Technician (EMT) with Alpha Community Ambulance Service, Inc., now Centre LifeLink EMS. During her last year of service to Alpha, she was selected to be an officer-in-charge (OIC), helping the organization earn its national accreditation status. Kerry responded to hundreds of EMS calls during her 5 years as an EMT, most notably the HUB Lawn sniper incident in 1996, during which she provided emergency care to one of the shooting victims. It was this incident that sparked Kerry's interest in the field of enhancing mental performance during stressful emergency situations. Her medical school education at the Philadelphia College of Osteopathic Medicine, internal medicine residency experience at Mercy Hospital of Pittsburgh, and current academic internist responsibilities have all deepened Kerry's commitment to teaching EMS personnel about how they can maintain mental toughness during medical emergencies. While Kerry has published articles about various topics in the fields of nutrition and medicine, *Code Calm on the Streets* is her first book.

E-MAIL: emscodecalm@gmail.com

MICHAEL J. ASKEN, PH.D.

Mike holds a B.A. degree in social & behavioral sciences from the Johns Hopkins University. He completed his doctoral degree in clinical psychology with a minor in medical psychology at West Virginia University and received his internship training at the East Orange (New Jersey) Veterans' Administration Hospital. He is a Fellow of the Division of Health Psychology and the Division of Exercise and Sport Psychology of the American Psychological Association.

He was involved in training physicians, intensive care unit nurses, neonatal intensive care unit nurses, nurse anesthetists and enterostomal therapists for twenty-five years. He was the psychologist for the Family Practice Residency at Polyclinic Medical Center and continues as the psychologist for Internal Medicine Residency and Surgical Residency Programs in Harrisburg, Pennsylvania. He was an adjunct assistant professor of behavioral science at the Milton S. Hershey Medical Center— Pennsylvania State University College of Medicine.

He has been an invited reviewer for Pennsylvania Medicine, the Journal of the American Medical Association, the Western Journal of Medicine, the Sport Psychologist, and Adapted Physical Activity Quarterly. Dr. Asken has published articles in the American Journal of Psychiatry, the Journal of Surgical Research, Primary Care, Journal of Family Practice, Pennsylvania Medicine, Journal of Medical Education, Family Medicine, Physician Executive, Journal of the Association of Nurse Anesthetists, Journal of Practical Nursing, Professional Psychology, the International Journal of Sport Psychology and Rehabilitation Psychology, among others.

While continuing to train residents and physicians, Dr. Asken is now the psychologist for the Pennsylvania State Police. He is on the editorial board of the The FireArms Instructor. He has written articles for PoliceOne.com., The Crisis Negotiator, The Tactical Edge, Calibre Press Street Survival Newsline, SWAT Digest, Law Officer, The Bulletin of the Pennsylvania Chiefs of Police, and the FireArms Instructor. He is an instructor for Top Gun undercover narcotics agent training. He has consulted with and/or provided training for the National Tactical Officers' Association, Eastern States Vice Investigators Association, the International Association of Law Enforcement Firearms Instructors, the New England Crisis Negotiator's Association, the FBI, the Pennsylvania Attorney General's Agents, the United States Postal Inspection Service, Navy Special Warfare Group I, and the U.S. Army War College.

Dr. Asken is the author of *MindSighting: Mental Toughness Skills for Police Officers in High Stress Situation* and *Emotional Intel: Mental Toughness Skills for High Stress Crisis Negotiations*. He is co-author with Lt. Colonel Dave Grossman and Loren Christensen of *Warrior MindSet: Mental Toughness Skills for a Nation's Defenders—Applying Performance Psychology to Combat*.

E-mail: dxrxtx@aol.com

41130541R00049

Made in the USA
Middletown, DE
04 March 2017